This fun phonics reader

belongs to

_____

Contents

Cover illustration by David Semple

A catalogue record for this book is available from the British Library

Published by Ladybird Books Ltd
27 Wrights Lane London W8 5TZ
A Penguin Company

2 4 6 8 10 9 7 5 3 1

© LADYBIRD BOOKS LTD MM

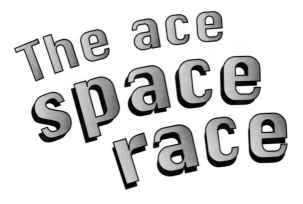

The ace space race

by Clive Gifford
illustrated by David Semple

introduces the 'magic e' spelling of
the long **a** vowel sound, as in name

Jake made a spaceship.

Kate made one, too.

They had a race in outer space.

Kate set off in a blaze of flames.

Jake had space to overtake!

Jake's spaceship led the chase.

But Kate raced past to take first place!

And now Kate's name
is in the Hall of Fame.

Home
sweet
home

by Dick Crossley
illustrated by Sue King

introduces the 'magic e' spelling of
the long **o** vowel sound, as in mole

Mole swung on the rope,

and ran up the slope.

Mole dived down the hole,

and slid down the pole.

Mole wrote out a note,

and pushed the door closed.

Mole unplugged the phone,
to be all alone.

Home, sweet home

in his hole, sweet hole…

a happy mole.

Nice Mike
and
Rude Jude

by Clive Gifford
illustrated by Kath Walker

introduces the 'magic e' spelling of the
long **i** and **u** vowel sounds, as in bike
and cube

This is Nice Mike,

who is always polite.

This is Rude Jude,

whom nobody likes.

Jude thinks it is cute
to act like a brute.

He makes Mike wipe
and shine his shoes.

He takes Mike's things:

his five white mice,

his kite,

his Silly Slime

and his nice
red bike.

But Nice Mike has a
surprise for Rude Jude.

phonics

Learn to read with Ladybird

phonics is one strand of Ladybird's **Learn to Read** range. It can be used alongside any other reading programme, and is an ideal way to support the reading work that your child is doing, or about to do, in school.

This chart will help you to pick the right book for your child from Ladybird's three main **Learn to Read** series.

Age	Stage	Phonics	Read with Ladybird	Read it yourself
4-5 years	Starter reader	Books 1-3	Level 1	Level 1
5-6 years	Developing reader	Books 2-9	Level 1-2	Level 2-3
6-7 years	Improving reader	Books 10-12	Level 2-3	Level 3-4
7-8 years	Confident reader		Level 3-4	Level 4

Ladybird has been a leading publisher of reading programmes for the last fifty years. **phonics** combines this experience with the latest research to provide a rapid route to reading success.

It's Mike's big brother,
Huge Bruce.